James Whitcomb Riley

The Old Swimmin'-Hole

Poems

James Whitcomb Riley

The Old Swimmin'-Hole
Poems

ISBN/EAN: 9783337006310

Printed in Europe, USA, Canada, Australia, Japan

Cover: Foto ©Thomas Meinert / pixelio.de

More available books at **www.hansebooks.com**

"The Old Swimmin'-hole,"

AND

'Leven More Poems,

BY

Benj. F. Johnson, of Boone.

[James Whitcomb Riley.]

SIXTH EDITION.

INDIANAPOLIS:
The Bowen-Merrill Co., Publishers and Booksellers.
1883.

PREFACE.

*A*S FAR BACK into boyhood as the writer's memory may intelligently go, the "country poet" is most pleasantly recalled. He was, and is, as common as the "country fiddler," and as full of good old-fashioned music. Not a master of melody, indeed, but a poet, certainly—

"Who, through long days of labor,
  And nights devoid of ease,
Still heard in his soul the music
  Of wonderful melodies."

And it is simply the purpose of this series of dialectic Studies to reflect the real worth of this homely child of Nature, and to echo faithfully, if possible, the faltering music of his song.

INDIANAPOLIS, Ind.,   J. W. R.
  July, 1883.

CONTENTS.

THE OLD SWIMMIN'-HOLE AND 'LEVEN MORE POEMS.

THE OLD SWIMMIN'-HOLE.

Oh! the old swimmin'-hole! whare the
    crick so still and deep
Looked like a baby-river that was laying
    half asleep,
And the gurgle of the worter round the
    drift jest below
Sounded like the laugh of something we
    onc't ust to know
Before we could remember anything but
    the eyes
Of the angels lookin' out as we left Para-
    dise;
But the merry days of youth is beyond our
    control,
And it's hard to part ferever with the old
    swimmin'-hole.

Oh! the old swimmin'-hole! In the happy
   days of yore,
When I ust to lean above it on the old
   sickamore,
Oh! it showed me a face in its warm sunny
   tide
That gazed back at me so gay and glorified,
It made me love myself, as I leaped to ca-
   ress
My shadder smilin' up at me with such
   tenderness.
But them days is past and gone, and old
   Time's tuck his toll
From the old man come back to the old
   swimmin'-hole.

Oh! the old swimmin'-hole! In the long,
   lazy days
When the hum-drum of school made so
   many run-a-ways,
How plesant was the jurney down the old
   dusty lane,
Whare the tracks of our bare feet was all
   printed so plain
You could tell by the dent of the heel and
   the sole
They was lots o' fun on hands at the old
   swimmin'-hole.

But the lost joys is past! Let your tears in
  sorrow roll
Like the rain that ust to dapple up the old
  swimmin'-hole.

Thare the bullrushes growed, and the cat-
  tails so tall,
And the sunshine and shadder fell over it
  all;
And it mottled the worter with amber and
  gold
Till the glad lilies rocked in the ripples
  that rolled;
And the snake-feeder's four gauzy wings
  fluttered by
Like the ghost of a daisy dropped out of
  the sky,
Or a wownded apple-blossom in the breeze's
  control,
As it cut acrost some orchard to'rds the old
  swimmin'-hole.

Oh! the old swimmin'-hole! When I last
  saw the place,
The scenes was all changed, like the
  change in my face;
The bridge of the railroad now crosses the
  spot

Whare the old divin'-log lays sunk and
  fergot.
And I stray down the banks whare the
  trees ust to be—
But never again will their shade shelter
  me!
And I wish in my sorrow I could strip to
  the soul,
And dive off in my grave like the old
  swimmin'-hole.

THOUGHTS FER THE DISCURAGED
FARMER.

THE summer winds is sniffin' round the
  bloomin' locus' trees;
And the clover in the pastur' is a big day
  fer the bees,
And they been a-swiggin' honey above
  board and on the sly,
Till they stutter in their buzzin', and stagger
  as they fly.
The flicker on the fence-rail pears to jest
  spit on his wings
And roll up his feathers by the sassy way
  he sings.
And the hossfly is a-whettin-up his fore
  legs fer biz
And the off-mare is a-switchin' all of her
  tale they is

You can hear the blackbirds jawin' as they
  foller up the plow—
Oh theyr bound to git theyr livin'
  and they don't care how

So they quarrel in the furries, and they
　　quarrel on the wing—
But theyr peaceabler in pot-pies than any
　　other thing:
And its when I git my shotgun drawed up
　　in stiddy rest,
She's as full of tribbelation as a yaller-
　　jacket's nest;
And a few shots before dinner, when the
　　sun's a-shinin' right,　　　　　.
Seems to kindo-sorto sharpen up a feller's
　　appetite!

They's been a heap o' rain, but the sun's
　　out to-day,
And the clouds of the wet spell is all
　　cleared away,
And the woods is all the greener, and the
　　grass is greener still;
It may rain again to-morry, but I don't
　　think it will.
Some says the crops is ruined, and the corn's
　　drownded out,
And propha-sy the wheat will be a failure,
　　without doubt;
But the kind Providence that has never
　　failed us yet,

Will be on hands onc't more at the 'leventh
  hour, I bet!

Does the medder-lark complain, as he swims
  high and dry
Through the waves of the wind and the
  blue of the sky?
Does the quail set up and whistle in a dis-
  appinted way,
Er hang his head in silence, and sorrow all
  the day?
Is the chipmuck's health a-failin'? Does
  he walk, er does he run?
Don't the buzzards ooze around up thare
  jest like they've allus done?
Is they anything the matter with the
  rooster's lungs er voice?
Ort a mortal be complainin' when dumb
  animals rejoice?

Then let us, once and all, be contented with
  our lot;
The June is here this morning, and the sun
  is shining hot.
Oh! let us fill our harts up with the glory
  of the day,

And banish ev'ry doubt and care and sor-
  row far away!
Whatever be our station, with Providence
  fer guide,
Such fine circumstances ort to make us
  satisfied;
Fer the world is full of roses, and the roses
  full of dew,
And the dew is full of heavenly love that
  drips fer me and you.

A SUMMER'S DAY.

THE Summer's put the idy in
My head that I'm a boy again;
   And all around's so bright and gay
   I want to put my team away,
   And jest git out whare I can lay
   And soak my hide full of the day!
But work is work, and must be done—
Yet, as I work, I have my fun,
Jest fancyin' these furries here
Is childhood's paths onc't more so dear:—
And so I walk through medder-lands,
   And country lanes, and swampy trails
Whare long bullrushes bresh my hands;
   And, tilted on the ridered rails
     Of deadnin' fences, "Old Bob White"
     Whistles his name in high delight,
And whirrs away. I wunder still,
Whichever way a boy's feet will—
Whare trees has fell, with tangled tops
   Whare dead leaves shakes, I stop fer
Heerin' the acorn as it drops—   [breth,
   H'istin' my chin up still as deth,

And watchin' clos't, with upturned eyes,
The tree whare Mr. Squirrel tries
To hide hisse'f above the limb,
But lets his own tale tell on him.

I wunder on in deeper glooms—
    Git hungry, hearin' female cries
From old farm-houses, whare perfumes
    Of harvest dinners seem to rise
And ta'nt a feller, hart and brane,
With memories he can't explain.

I wunder through the underbresh,
    Whare pig-tracks, pintin' to'rds the crick
Is picked and printed in the fresh
    Black-bottom lands, like wimmern pick
Their pie-crusts with a fork, some way,
When bakin' fer camp-meetin' day.

I wunder on and on and on,
Till my gray hair and beard is gone,
And every wrinkle on my brow
Is rubbed clean out, and shaddered now
With curls as brown and fair and fine
As tenderls of the wild grape-vine
That ust to climb the highest tree
To keep the ripest ones fer me.
I wunder still, and here I am
Wadin' the ford below the dam—

The worter chucklin' round my knee
   At hornet-welt and bramble scratch,
And me a-slippin' 'crost to see
   Ef Tyner's plums is ripe, and size
The old man's wortermelon-patch,
   With juicy mouth and drouthy eyes.
Then, after sich a day of mirth
And happiness as worlds is worth—
   So tired that heaven seems nigh about,—
The sweetest tiredness on earth
   Is to git home and flatten out—
So tired you can't lay flat enough,
And sort o' wish that you could spred
Out like molasses on the bed,
And jest drip off the aidges in
The dreams that never comes again.

A HYMB OF FAITH.

O, THOU that doth all things devise
    And fashion fer the best,
Help us who sees with mortal eyes
    To overlook the rest.

They's times, of course, we grope in doubt,
    And in affliction sore;
So knock the louder, Lord, without,
    And we'll unlock the door.

Make us to feel, when times looks bad
    And tears in pitty melts,
Thou wast the only help we had
    When they was nothin' else.

Death comes alike to ev'ry man
    That ever was borned on earth;
Then let us do the best we can
    To live for all life 's worth.

Ef storms and tempests dread to see
    Makes black the heavens o'er,

They done the same in Galillee,
   Two thousand years before.

But, after all, the golden sun
   Poured out its floods on them
That watched and waited fer the One
   Then borned in Bethlyham.

Also, the star of holy writ
   Made noonday of the night,
While other stars that looked at it
   Was envious with delight.

The sages then in worship bowed,
   From every clime so fare;
O, sinner, think of that glad crowd
   That congregated thare!

They was content to fall in ranks
   With One that knowed the way
From good old Jurden's stormy banks
   Clean up to Judgment Day.

No matter, then, how all is mixed
   In our near-sighted eyes,
All things is fer the best, and fixed
   Out straight in Paradise.

Then take things as God sends 'em here,
  And, ef we live or die,
Be more and more contenteder,
  Without a-asking why.

O, thou that doth all things devise
  And fashion fer the best,
Help us who sees with mortal eyes
  To overlook the rest.

OLD worter-melon time is a-comin' round
    again,
    And they ain't no man a-livin' any tick-
    leder'n me,
Fer the way I hanker after worter-melons
    is a sin—
    Which is the why and wharefore, as you
    can plainly see.

Oh, it's in the sandy soil worter-melons
    does the best,
    And its thare they'll lay and waller in
    the sunshine and the dew
Till they wear all the green streaks clean
    off of theyr breast,
    And you bet I ain't a-findin' any fault
    with them; air you?

They ain't no better thing in the vegetable
    line;
    And they don't need much 'tendin', as
    ev'ry farmer knows;

And when theyr ripe and ready fer to
    pluck from the vine,
      I want to say to you theyr the best fruit
      that grows.

It's some likes the yaller-core, and some
    likes the red,
      And it's some says "The little Californy"
      is the best;
But the sweetest slice of all I ever wedged
    in my head,
      Is the old "Edingburg Mounting-sprout,"
      of the west.

You don't want no punkins nigh your wor-
    ter-melon vines—
      'Cause, some-way-another, they'll spile
      your melons, shore;—
I've seed 'em taste like punkins, from the
    core to the rines,
      Which may be a fact you have heerd of
      before.

But your melons that's raised right, and
    'tended to with care,
      You can walk around amongst 'em with
      a parent's pride and joy,
And thump 'em on the heads with as
    fatherly a air

As ef each one of them was your little
girl er boy.

I joy in my hart jest to hear that rippin'
sound
When you split one down the back and
jolt the halves in two,
And the friends you love the best is geth-
ered all around—
And you says unto your sweetheart, "Oh
here's the core fer you!"

And I like to slice 'em up in big pieces fer
'em all,
Espeshally the children, and watch theyr
high delight
As one by one the rines with theyr pink
notches falls,
And they holler fer some more, with un-
quenched appetite.

Boys take to it natchural, and I like to see
'em eat—
A slice of worter-melon's like a french-
harp in theyr hands,
And when they "saw" it through theyr
mouth sich music can't be beat—
'Cause it's music both the sperit and the
stummick understands.

Oh, they's more in worter-melons than the
    purty-colored meat,
    And the overflowin' sweetness of the
    worter squashed betwixt
The up'ard and the down'ard motions of
    a feller's teeth,
    And it's the taste of ripe old age and
    juicy childhood mixed.

Fer I never taste a melon but my thoughts
    flies away
    To the summertime of youth, and again
    I see the dawn,
And the fadin' afternoon of the long sum-
    mer day,
    And the dusk and dew a-fallin', and the
    night a-comin' on.

And thare's the corn around us, and the
    lispin' leaves and trees,
    And the stars a-peekin' down on us as
    still as silver mice,
And us boys in the worter-melons on our
    hands and knees,
    And the new moon hangin' o'er us like a
    yaller-cored slice.

O, it's worter-melon time is a-comin' round
    again,

And they ain't no man a-livin' any tick-
   leder'n me,
Fer the way I hanker after worter-melons
   is a sin—
Which is the why and wharefore, as you
   can plainly see.

MY PHILOSOFY.

I AINT, ner don't p'tend to be,
Much posted on philosofy;
But thare is times, when all alone,
I work out idees of my own.
And of these same thare is a few
I'd like to jest refer to you—
Pervidin' that you don't object
To listen clos't and rickollect.

I allus argy that a man
Who does about the best he can
Is plenty good enough to suit
This lower mundane institute—
No matter ef his daily walk
Is subject fer his neghbor's talk,
And critic-minds of ev'ry whim
Jest all git up and go fer him!

I knowed a feller onc't that had
The yaller-janders mighty bad,
And each and ev'ry friend he'd meet
Would stop and give him a receet

Fer curin' of 'em. But he'd say
He kind o' thought they'd go away
Without no medicin', and boast
That he'd git well without one doste.

He kep' a yallerin' on—and they
Perdictin' that he'd die some day
Before he knowed it! Tuck his bed,
The feller did, and lost his head,
And wundered in his mind a spell—
Then rallied, and, at last, got well;
But ev'ry friend that said he'd die
Went back on him eternaly!

Its natchural enough, I guess,
When some gits more and some gits less,
Fer them-uns on the slimmest side
To claim it aint a fair divide;
And I've knowed some to lay and wait,
And git up soon, and set up late,
To ketch some feller they could hate
Fer goin' at a faster gait.

The signs is bad when folks commence
A findin' fault with Providence,
And balkin' 'cause the earth don't shake
At ev'ry prancin' step they take.

No man is great till he can see
How less than little he would be
Ef stripped to self, and stark and bare
He hung his sign out anywhare.

My doctern is to lay aside
Contensions, and be satisfied:
Jest do your best, and praise er blame
That follers that, counts jest the same.
I've allus noticed grate success
Is mixed with troubles, more or less
And its the man who does the best
That gits more kicks than all the rest

WHEN THE FROST IS ON THE PUNKIN.

WHEN the frost is on the punkin and the
fodder's in the shock,
And you hear the kyouck and gobble of
the struttin' turkey-cock,
And the clackin' of the guineys, and the
cluckin' of the hens,
And the rooster's hallylooyer as he tiptoes
on the fence;
O its then's the times a feller is a-feelin' at
his best,
With the risin' sun to greet him from a
night of peaceful rest,
As he leaves the house, bare-headed, and
goes out to feed the stock,
When the frost is on the punkin and the
fodder's in the shock.

They's something kindo' harty-like about
the atmosphere

When the heat of summer's over and the
coolin' fall is here—
Of course we miss the flowers, and the
blossoms on the trees,
And the mumble of the hummin'-birds
and buzzin' of the bees;
But the air's so appetizin'; and the land-
scape through the haze
Of a crisp and sunny morning of the airly
autumn days
Is a pictur' that no painter has the colorin'
to mock—
When the frost is on the punkin and the
fodder's in the shock.

The husky, rusty rustle of the tossels of the
corn,
And the raspin' of the tangled leaves, as
golden as the morn;
The stubble in the furries—kindo' lone-
some-like, but still
A-preachin' sermons to us of the barns they
growed to fill;
The strawstack in the medder, and the
reaper in the shed;
The hosses in theyr stalls below—the clover
overhead!—

O, it sets my heart a-clickin' like the tickin'
   of a clock,
When the frost is on the punkin and the
   fodder's in the shock!

ON THE DEATH OF LITTLE MAHALA ASHCRAFT.

"LITTLE HALY! Little Haly!" cheeps the
    robin in the tree;
"Little Haly!" sighs the clover, "Little
    Haly!" moans the bee;
"Little Haly! Little Haly!" calls the kill-
    deer at twilight;
And the katydids and crickets hollers
    "Haly" all the night.

The sunflowers and the hollyhawks droops
    over the garden fence;
The old path down the gardenwalks still
    holds her footprints' dents;
And the well-sweep's swingin' bucket seems
    to wait fer her to come
And start it on its wortery errant down the
    old bee-gum.

The bee-hives all is quiet, and the little
    Jersey steer,

When any one comes nigh it, acts so lone-
 some like and queer;
And the little Banty chickens kind o' cut-
 ters faint and low,
Like the hand that now was feedin' 'em
 was one they didn't know.

They's sorrow in the wavin' leaves of all
 the apple-trees;
And sorrow in the harvest-sheaves, and
 sorrow in the breeze;
And sorrow in the twitter of the swallers
 'round the shed;
And all the song her red-bird sings is "Lit-
 tle Haly's dead!"

The medder 'pears to miss her, and the
 pathway through the grass,
Whare the dewdrops ust to kiss her little
 bare feet as she passed;
And the old pin in the gate-post seems to
 kindo-sorto' doubt
That Haly's little sunburnt hands'll ever
 pull it out.

Did her father er her mother ever love her
 more'n me,
Er her sisters er her brother prize her love
 more tenderly?

I question—and what answer?—only tears,
and tears alone,
And ev'ry neghbor's eyes is full o' tear-
drops as my own.

"Little Haly! Little Haly!" cheeps the
robin in the tree;
"Little Haly!" sighs the clover, "Little
Haly!" moans the bee;
"Little Haly! Little Haly!" calls the kill-
deer at twilight,
And the katydids and crickets hollers
"Haly" all the night.

THE MULBERRY TREE.

O, ITS many's the scenes which is dear to
  my mind
As I think of my childhood so long left
  behind;
The home of my birth, with its old pun-
  cheon floor,
And the bright mornin'-glories that growed
  round the door;
The warped clab-board roof whare the rain
  it run off
Into streams of sweet dreams as I laid in
  the loft,
Countin' all of the joys that was dearest
  to me,
And a-thinkin' the most of the mulberry
  tree.

And to-day as I dream, with both eyes
  wide-awake,
I can see the old tree, and its limbs as they
  shake,

And the long purple berries that rained
  on the ground
Whare the pastur' was bald whare we
  trommped it around.
And again, peekin' up through the thick
  leafy shade,
I can see the glad smiles of the friends
  when I strayed
With my little bare feet from my own
  mother's knee
To foller them off to the mulberry tree.

Leanin' up in the forks, I can see the old
  rail,
And the boy climbin' up it, claw, tooth,
  and toe-nail,
And in fancy can hear, as he spits on his
  hands,
The ring of his laugh and the rip of his
  pants.
But that rail led to glory, as certain and
  shore
As I'll never climb thare by that rout' any
  more—
What was all the green laurels of Fame
  unto me,
With my brows in the boughs of the mul-
  berry tree?

Then its who can fergit the old mulberry
  tree
That he knowed in the days when his
  thoughts was as free
As the flutterin' wings of the birds that
  flew out
Of the tall wavin' tops as the boys come
  about?
O, a crowd of my memories, laughin' and
  gay,
Is a-climbin' the fence of that pastur' to-
  day,
And a pantin' with joy, as us boys ust to be,
They go racin' acrost fer the mulberry tree.

TO MY OLD NEGHBOR, WILLIAM LEACHMAN.

Fer forty year and better you have been a
    friend to me,
Through days of sore afflictions and dire
    adversity,
You allus had a kind word of counsel to
    impart,
Which was like a healin' 'intment to the
    sorrow of my hart.

When I burried my first womern, William
    Leachman, it was you
Had the only consolation that I could lis-
    ten to—
Fer I knowed you had gone through it and
    had rallied from the blow,
And when you said I'd do the same, I
    knowed you'd ort to know.

But that time I'll long remember; how I
    wundered here and thare—

Through the settin'-room and kitchen, and
  out in the open air—
And the snowflakes whirlin', whirlin', and
  the fields·a frozen glare,
And the neghbors' sleds and wagons con-
  gregatin ev'rywhare.

I turned my eyes to'rds heaven, but the
  sun was hid away;
I turned my eyes to'rds earth again, but
  all was cold and gray;
And the clock, like ice a-crackin', clickt
  the icy hours in two—
And my eyes'd never thawed out ef it
  hadn't been fer you!

We set thare by the smoke-house—me and
  you out thare alone—
Me a-thinkin'—you a-talkin' in a soothin'
  undertone—
You a-talkin'—me a-thinkin' of the sum-
  mers long ago,
And a-writin' "Marthy—Marthy" with my
  finger in the snow!

William Leachman, I can see you jest as
  plain as I could then;

And your hand is on my shoulder, and you
    rouse me up again;
And I see the tears a-drippin' from your
    own eyes, as you say:
"Be reconciled and bear it—we but linger
    fer a day!"

At the last Old Settlers' Meetin', we went
    j'intly, you and me—
Your hosses and my wagon, as you wanted
    it to be;
And sence I can remember, from the time
    we've neghbored here,
In all sich friendly actions you have double-
    done your sheer.

It was better than the meetin', too, that
    9-mile talk we had
Of the times when we first settled here and
    travel was so bad;
When we had to go on hoss-back, and
    sometimes on "Shanks's mare,"
And "blaze" a road fer them behind that
    had to travel thare.

And now we was a-trottin' 'long a leve'
    gravel pike,

In a big two-hoss road-wagon, jest as easy
as you like—
Two of us on the front seat, and our wim-
ern-folks behind,
A-settin' in their Winsor cheers in perfect
peace of mind!

And we pinted out old landmarks, nearly
faded out of sight:—
Thare they ust to rob the stage-coach; thare
Gash Morgan had the fight
With the old stag-deer that pronged him—
how he battled fer his life,
And lived to prove the story by the handle
of his knife.

Thare the first griss-mill was put up in the
settlement, and we
Had tuck our grindin' to it in the fall of
Forty-three—
When we tuck our rifles with us, techin'
elbows all the way,
And a-stickin' right together ev'ry minute,
night and day.

Thare ust to stand the tavern that they
called the "Travelers' Rest,"

And thare, beyent the covered bridge,
  "The Counterfitters' Nest"—
Whare they claimed the house was ha'nted
  —that a man was murdered thare,
And burried underneath the floor, er round
  the place somewhare.

And the old Plank Road they laid along in
  Fifty-one er two—
You know we talked about the times when
  that old road was new:
How "Uncle Sam" put down that road and
  never taxed the State
Was a problem, don't you rickollect, we
  couldn't dimonstrate?

Ways was devious, William Leachman, that
  me and you has past;
But as I found you true at first, I find you
  true at last,
And, now the time's a-comin' mighty nigh
  our jurney's end,
I want to throw wide open all my soul to
  you, my friend.

With the stren'th of all my bein', and the
  heat of hart and brane,

And ev'ry livn' drop of blood in artery
  and vane,
I love you and respect you, and I venerate
  your name,
Fer the name of William Leachman and
  True Manhood's jest the same!

MY FIDDLE.

My FIDDLE?—Well, I kindo' keep her handy,
    don't you know!
Though I aint so much inclined to tromp
    the strings and switch the bow
As I was before the timber of my elbows
    got so dry,
And my fingers was more limber-like and
    caperish and spry;
    Yet I can plonk and plunk and plink,
      And tune her up and play,
    And jest lean back and laugh and wink
      At ev'ry rainy day!

My playin's only middlin'—tunes I picked
    up when a boy—
The kindo'-sorto' fiddlin, that the folks
    calls "cordaroy;"
"The Old Fat Gal," and "Rye-straw," and
    "My Sailyor's on the Sea,"
Is the old cowtillions I "saw" when the
    ch'ice is left to me;

And so I plunk and plonk and plink,
  And rosum-up my bow,
And play the tunes that makes you think
  The devil's in your toe!

I was allus a romancin', do-less boy, to tell
    the truth,
A-fiddlin' and a-dancin', and a wastin of
    my youth,
And a actin' and a cuttin'-up all sorts o'
    silly pranks
That wasn't worth a button of anybody's
    thanks!
  But they tell me, when I ust to plink
    And plonk and plunk and play,
  My music seemed to have the kink
    O' drivin' cares away!

That's how this here old fiddle's won my
    hart's indurin' love!
From the strings acrost her middle to the
    schreechin' keys above—
From her "apern," over bridge, and to the
    ribbon round her throat,
She's a wooin', cooin' pigeon, singin' "Love
    me" ev'ry note!

And so I pat her neck, and plink
   Her strings with lovin' hands,
And, list'nin' clos't, I sometimes think
   She kindo' understands!

THE CLOVER.

Some sings of the lily, and daisy, and rose,
And the pansies and pinks that the sum-
    mertime throws
In the green grassy lap of the medder that
    lays
Blinkin' up at the skyes through the sun-
    shiny days;
But what is the lily, and all of the rest
Of the flowers, to a man with a hart in his
    breast
That was dipped brimmin' full of the honey
    and dew
Of the sweet clover-blossoms his babyhood
    knew?

I never set eyes on a clover-field now,
Er fool round a stable, er climb in the mow,
But my childhood comes back jest as clear
    and as plain
As the smell of the clover I'm sniffin'
    again;
And I wunder away in a bare-footed dream,

Whare I tangle my toes in the blossoms
    that gleam
With the dew of the dawn of the morning
    of love
Ere it wept o'er the graves that I'm weepin'
    above.

Aud so I love clover—it seems like a part
Of the sacredest sorrows and joys of my
    hart;
And wharever it blossoms, oh, tharo let me
    bow
And thank the good God as I'm thankin'
    Him now;
And I pray to Him still for the stren'th,
    when I die,
To go out in the clover and tell it good-bye,
And lovin'ly nestle my face in its bloom
While my soul slips away on a breth of
    perfume.

THE END.

www.ingramcontent.com/pod-product-compliance
Lightning Source LLC
Chambersburg PA
CBHW032134080426
42733CB00008B/1069